THE CLOUDED HILLS

p.36,38,39

p.20

p.24

MYSTICISM AND MODERN MAN

The Clouded Hills

Selections from William Blake

edited by Catharine Hughes

Sheed & Ward

NEW YORK   LONDON

The quotations are from the edition of Blake's complete writings edited by Geoffrey Keynes, published by the Nonesuch Press, London, and Random House, New York.

Library of Congress Catalog Card Number 73-2371

All that can happen to Man is his pilgrimage of seventy years.

Every Night & every Morn   **3**
Some to Misery are Born.
Every Morn & every Night
Some are Born to sweet delight.
Some are Born to sweet delight,
Some are Born to Endless Night.

2

4

Seek Love in the Pity of others' Woe,
In the gentle relief of another's care,
In the darkness of night & the winter's snow,
In the naked & outcast, Seek Love there!

Think of a white cloud as being holy, you cannot love it; but think of a holy man within the cloud, love springs up in your thoughts, for to think of holiness distinct from man is impossible to the affections. Thought alone can make monsters, but the affections cannot.

7

Do what you will, this life's a fiction
And is made up of contradiction.

If you have form'd a Circle to go into,
Go into it yourself & see how you would do.

Amaz'd & in fear
I each particle gazed,
Astonish'd, Amazed;
For each was a Man
Human-form'd. Swift I ran,
For they beckon'd to me
Remote by the Sea,
Saying: "Each grain of Sand,
Every Stone on the Land,
Each rock & each hill,
Each fountain & rill,
Each herb & each tree,
Mountain, hill, earth & sea,
Cloud, Meteor & Star,
Are Men seen Afar."

To see a World in a Grain of Sand
And a Heaven in a Wild Flower,
Hold Infinity in the palm of your hand
And Eternity in an hour.

10

Can I see another's woe,
And not be in sorrow too?
Can I see another's grief,
And not seek for kind relief?

Can I see a falling tear,
And not feel my sorrow's share?
Can a father see his child
Weep, nor be with sorrow fill'd?

Think not thou canst sigh a sigh
And thy maker is not by;
Think not thou canst weep a tear
And thy maker is not near.

Little Lamb, who made thee?
Dost thou know who made thee?
Gave thee life, & bid thee feed
By the stream & o'er the mead;
Gave thee clothing of delight,
Softest clothing, wooly, bright;
Gave thee such a tender voice,
Making all the vales rejoice?
Little Lamb, who made thee?
Dost thou know who made thee?

Little Lamb, I'll tell thee,
Little Lamb, I'll tell thee:
He is called by thy name,
For he calls himself a Lamb.
He is meek, & he is mild;
He became a little child.
I a child, & thou a lamb,
We are called by his name,
Little Lamb, God bless thee!
Little Lamb, God bless thee!

If the doors of perception were cleansed every
thing would appear to man as it is, infinite.
    For man has closed himself up, till he sees
all things thro' narrow chinks of his cavern.

And did the Countenance Divine
Shine forth upon our clouded hills?
And was Jerusalem builded here
Among these dark Satanic Mills?

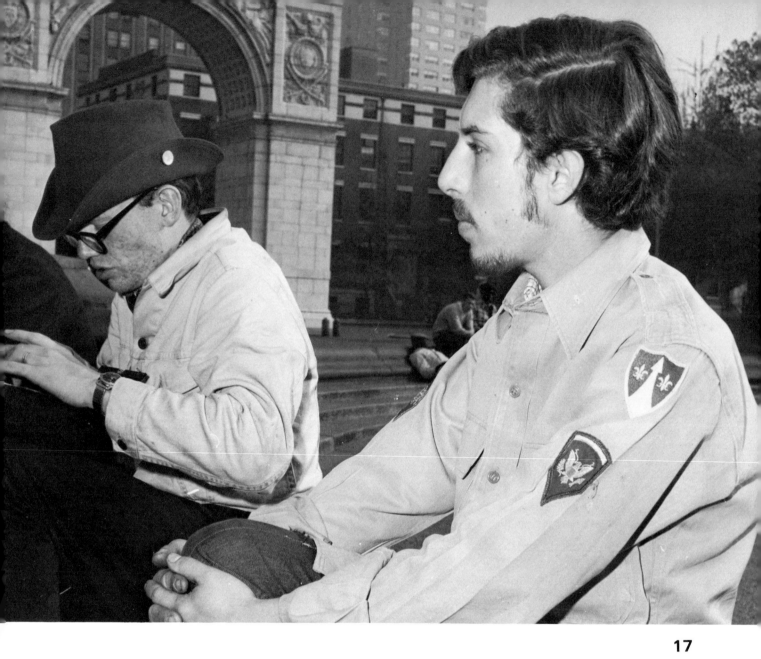

17

18

"Father, O Father! what do we here
In this Land of unbelief & fear?
The Land of Dreams is better far,
Above the light of the Morning Star."

The inhabitants are sick to death: they labour
    to divide into Days
And Nights the uncertain Periods, and into
    Weeks & Months. In vain
They send the Dove & Raven & in vain the
    Serpent over the mountains
And in vain the Eagle & Lion over the four-fold
    wilderness:
They return not, but generate in rocky places
    desolate:
They return not, but build a habitation
    separate from Man.

Sacrifice the Parts, What becomes of the Whole?

O what is Life & what is Man? O what is
      Death? Wherefore
Are you, my Children, natives in the Grave to
      where I go?

Or are you born to feed the hungry ravenings
      of Destruction.
To be the sport of Accident, to waste in Wrath
      & Love a weary
Life, in brooking cares & anxious labours that
      prove but chaff?

To Mercy, Pity, Peace, and Love
All pray in their distress;
And to these virtues of delight
Return their thankfulness.

For Mercy, Pity, Peace, and Love
Is God, our father dear,
And Mercy, Pity, Peace, and Love
Is Man, his child and care.

For Mercy has a human heart,
Pity a human face,
And, Love, the human form divine,
And Peace, the human dress.

Then every man, of every clime,
That prays in his distress,
Prays to the human form divine,
Love, Mercy, Pity, Peace.

And all must love the human form,
In heathen, turk, or jew;
Where Mercy, Love, & Pity dwell
There God is dwelling too.

23

The Vision of Christ that thou dost see
Is my Vision's Greatest Enemy:

. . . .

Thine is the friend of all Mankind,
Mine speaks in parables to the Blind:
Thine loves the same world that mine hates,
Thy Heaven doors are my Hell gates.

He who doubts from what he sees
Will ne'er Believe, do what you Please.
If the Sun & Moon should doubt,
They'd immediately Go out.

Thought is act. Christ's acts were nothing to
Caesar's if this is not so.

27   Men are admitted into Heaven not because
they have curbed & govern'd their Passions,
or have no Passions, but because they have
cultivated their Understandings.

Passion & Expression is Beauty Itself. The Face that is Incapable of Passion & Expression is deformity Itself. Let it be Painted & Patch'd & Praised & Advertised for Ever, it will only be admired by Fools.

Man can have no idea of any thing greater than Man, as a cup cannot contain more than its capaciousness. But God is a man, not because he is so perceiv'd by man, but because he is the creator of man.

In every cry of every man,
In every Infant's cry of fear,
In every voice, in every ban,
The mind-forg'd manacles I hear.

What is fortune but an outward accident, for
a few years . . . and then gone?

31

32

As the Pilgrim passes while the Country
permanent remains,
So Men pass on, but States remain permanent
for ever.

For all are Men in Eternity, Rivers, Mountains,
       Cities, Villages,
All are Human, & when you enter into their
       Bosoms you walk
In Heavens & Earths, as in your own Bosom
       you bear your Heaven
And Earth & all you behold; tho' it appears
       Without, it is Within,
In your Imagination, of which this World of
       Mortality is but a Shadow.

If you trap the moment before it's ripe,
The tears of repentance you'll certainly wipe;
But if once you let the ripe moment go
You can never wipe off the tears of woe.

Silence remain'd & every one resum'd his
       Human Majesty.
And many conversed on these things as they
       labour'd at the furrow,
Saying: "It is better to prevent misery than
       to release from misery:
It is better to prevent error than to forgive
       the criminal.
Labour well the Minute Particulars, attend
       to the Littleones,
And those who are in misery cannot remain
       so long
If we do but our duty: labour well the teeming
       Earth."

Cruelty has a Human Heart,
And Jealousy a Human Face;
Terror the Human Form Divine,
And Secrecy the Human Dress.

The Human Dress is forged Iron,
The Human Form a fiery Forge,
The Human Face a Furnace seal'd,
The Human Heart its hungry Gorge.

"Come, O thou Lamb of God, and take away
        the remembrance of Sin.
To Sin & to hide the Sin in sweet deceit
        is lovely!
To Sin in the open face of day is cruel &
        pitiless! But
To record the Sin for a reproach, to let the
        Sun go down
In a remembrance of the Sin, is a Woe & a
        Horror,
A brooder of an Evil Day and a Sun rising
        in blood!
Come then, O Lamb of God, and take away
        the remembrance of Sin."

Every Eye sees differently. As the Eye, Such
The Object.

Both read the Bible day & night,
But thou read'st black where I read white.

39

The increase of a State, as of a man, is from internal improvement or intellectual acquirement. Man is not improved by the hurt of another. States are not improved at the expense of foreigners.

40

42

Great things are done when Men & Mountains
        meet;
This is not done by Jostling in the Street.

He who mocks the Infant's Faith
Shall be mock'd in Age & Death.
He who shall teach the Child to Doubt
The rotting Grave shall ne'er get out.

43

we are put on earth a little space,
That we may learn to bear the beams of love.

WILLIAM BLAKE

"There are some men, of great personality and power, who seem by some mistake of the divinities to have been dropped on the right planet but at the wrong time, or to have arrived at the right time but on the wrong planet," wrote J. B. Priestley in 1960, "and Blake is one of them. . . . Probably his own time has still to come."

But time passes ever so quickly. Less than a dozen years after Priestley's observations, Blake's work not only had enjoyed a major resurgence but provided the basis for a play at the British National Theatre. "Artist, writer and seer" (as Priestley described him), he is increasingly read and responded to, particularly by the young. Once viewed as insane, he is today regarded as a mystic, a poet of the soul.

William Blake was born in London on November 28, 1757. His father apprenticed him to an engraver. It was a talent that was to come in handy, for many of his early lyric and prophetic poems were etched on copper plates by Blake and printed by him and his wife.

Blake was a self-taught and seemingly a "difficult" man, a rebel—a fact that obviously lends him much of his appeal for the readers of today. He supported the American and French revolutions, was a friend of Tom Paine. His later poems, however, became much less political, much more religious, notably in *The Four Zoas*, *Milton* and *Jerusalem*.

Poor, with the reputation of "Christian hermit," in the last years of his life Blake became almost a cult figure for "saintly young men." But his religious rebellion was as genuine—as "matter-of-fact"—as his earlier political one. In both spheres he was a "heretic." "God to Blake personified absolute authority," says J. Bronowski in an introduction to Blake's work in the Penguin Poets series, "and Christ personified the human character; and Blake was on the side of man against authority."

Blake's other major works include *Songs of Innocence, Songs of Experience, The Marriage of Heaven and Hell* and *The Book of Thel*. He died in London on August 12, 1827, a prophet certainly not honored in his time, very much a prophet for our time.